M000023155

QUICK AND EASY WAYS TO KICK-START A SUCCESSFUL MICROBLADING BUSINESS . . .

EVEN IF YOU HAVE NO MARKETING OR SALES EXPERIENCE

Copyright © 2010 All rights reserved.

This book or any portion thereof
may not be reproduced or used in any manner whatsoever
without the express written permission of the publisher
except for the use of brief quotations in a book review.

Printed in the United States of America

Table of Contents

CHAPTER 1

---※---

What Do You Need to Start a Microblading Career?

Getting your salon set up properly for microblading is an essential part of running a business. Microblading is more than just your average haircut, so there are a few extra steps you'll need to take in order protect yourself and your clients, as opposed to running a regular salon.

Your first step is to get a license. Check with the local Department of Health to find out exactly what licenses you require. At the very least, you'll probably need a permanent cosmetic practitioner or tattoo license or a body art practitioner and a blood borne pathogen certification.

Choose the Right Microblading Tools

Pick the best microblading tools and pigments available in the market. Experts recommend Phibrows products to ensure your customers will have the best results and these products are the industry standard.

Microblading Pen: Microblading techniques require a manual microblading pen, not a permanent makeup machine. The pen will allow you to make the most natural hair strokes possible, whereas the machine is super hard to control. We recommend using the disposable pens since these are the safest option for clients. You can dispose of them after every client, providing a safe procedure to prevent any infections or negative feedback and reviews.

Pigments: You'll need pigments in various colors on an ongoing basis. Start out with the most popular colors and select hues that you can mix to get just the right shade for your clients. As you build your business, you can expand what you offer. It's essential that you use the absolute best pigments to avoid the healed results turning blue, gray, or red.

Anesthetics: You want clients to feel as much comfortable as possible. That is why you should use anesthetics during the microblading procedure to prevent pain, swelling, and discomfort. Use a safe numbing solution. Most anesthetics include lidocaine for during the process. Remember to do a patch test beforehand so you will not have any complications later.

Needles: Again, these are an ongoing expense, and you'll want to stock up on high-quality needles to avoid potential issues in the future. Make sure the needles are sterilized with lot number and sterilization expiration date. Disposables are recommended. These will come packaged individually and should only be opened immediately before you are ready to start the procedure.

Your local health department may have other requirements for your salon space, as well. Be sure to check.

You can check out all Phibrows products in the USA at:www.usamicroblading.com/shop

Other tools and ongoing expenses include:

Microblading Bed: You can use a facial bed, waxing bed, or a massage bed. Make sure that they fit your room and are also visually appealing. These beds need to have a smooth surface, as required by the health department.

Chair: Make sure the chair has a smooth surface as required by the health department. It should be nice and easy to clean, as well as visually appealing.

Light: There's no way you can do microblading without proper lighting. You need to make sure the light is bright enough for you to see the hair strokes, especially on clients with a lot of eyebrow hair.

This is an important area that you cannot overlook. In our experience, the Glamcor Light Elite 2 is the best not only for microblading but also for eyelash extensions. This is our opinion after trying a wide variety of lights. If you cannot see, you will make double strokes and the strokes will not look like real hair but will look big and unnatural.

Sink: Install a sink in the microblading area as required by most health officials. This will ensure you can wash your hands before and after each microblading procedure to prevent cross-contamination.

Sharps Container: Make sure you have a mail back system sharps container to dispose of used needles as required by health departments. This should be clearly labeled as such. You will need red biohazard bags to use with the sharps container.

Sterilization Materials:

- Sani Cloth for sterilization of tools
- Barrier film tape to cover lamp or a permanent makeup machine

- Alcohol antiseptic to clean and disinfect client's brows before the procedure
- Hairnet for client and artist
- A dental bib to cover working surfaces
- Face mask
- Disposable gloves
- Disposable blades

For a complete list of required sterilization materials, visit website: www.usamicroblading.com/sterilizationlist

CHAPTER 2

HOW TO AVOID BEING SUED

One of the risks of having a microblading business, or any service business, for that matter, is an unhappy customer. What do you do if someone isn't pleased with your work? In today's litigation-happy world, you have two choices.

First, avoid doing anything wrong in the first place. You should have systems in place to ensure you can prove that you are in the right. This includes surveillance systems and photos if need be.

Follow all guidelines and regulations to be sure you are not in violation of any of the rules in your area. A client may be unhappy, but if you haven't violated any rules or regulations, they will not be able to do much about it. In addition, you'll take steps to make them happier about it.

The second method is to make good on any mistakes or perceived mistakes. For example, if a customer isn't happy with your work, you could offer a discount or provide a redo. Doing what you can to fix the problem will go a long way toward preventing a lawsuit.

Consent Form

You also need to have client sign a thorough **consent form** before any procedure. Since this is a somewhat invasive procedure, you'll need a consent form before you start working on someone's brows. You should have your lawyer create a comprehensive form for you, but the consent form must include all medical history, age, and explanations of all of what to expect from the microblading procedure to make sure the client understands the whole process. In most states, you must keep the consent forms for 2 to 3 years.

Your consent form needs to include the following

Possible risks and complications: Explain clearly what regular reactions and healing processes look like, as well as what other effects may occur.

Allergy notifications: Require the client to let you know if they are allergic to anything you are using, including pigments, needles, and anesthesia.

Health concerns and diseases: Your client should notify you if they have any bloodborne diseases so you can take appropriate precautions, but you will also need to know if they have a health condition that may cause issues with the procedure.

Aftercare instructions: Give them instructions on how to look after the site once the microblading is complete.

Normal changes: Inform the client of the possibility that pigments may change slightly in color over time and let them know that this is not grounds for free treatments.

Things to avoid: Let the client know that certain skin treatments could cause the eyebrows to change color, fade, or look different. It's important to let them know that this is not your responsibility and that they need to inform anyone doing another procedure that they have had microblading done.

Medical care: The client should acknowledge that if they notice any adverse effects, they should seek medical care immediately.

The client should also confirm in writing that they have read the information regarding aftercare and risks and complications and understand it all. Again, having a lawyer create this document for you is important to ensure you are protected from liability.

Starting a business is a big endeavor and requires some planning ahead. Above all, make sure you have all your legal ducks in a row, to prevent issues in the future.

For a copy of thorough consent form with medical histories, visit: www.usamicroblading.com/consentform

Aftercare

You also must provide aftercare instructions form and have client sign the form to indicate that the client understands fully how to take proper care of their eyebrows as they heal, and once healing is complete.

Ins and Outs of Insurance

Every salon should have insurance, but if you are offering microblading, it's even more important. Should something go wrong, you'll need insurance that protects you against liability claims, as well as the usual theft, disasters, and property damages that might occur.

After you've worked so hard to get your business started, you don't want to lose it all over a simple fire or a disgruntled customer. Research comprehensive cosmetic tattoo insurance to be certain you are completely covered.

Keep in mind that some insurance companies are very picky about who they sell insurance to. They will want to know where you were licensed and what sort of training you've had. Your standing with the health department will also come into play, and you will need to meet specific requirements (depending on the insurance company) to get insured.

The typical cost of insurance for microblading is around $800 per year. If you charge $500 per service, you can afford $800 a year for insurance. If you want insurance resources, please check out www.usamicroblading.com/insurance to choose where you can buy insurance.

CHAPTER 3

HOW TO BUILD YOUR IMAGE FOR BUSINESS SUCCESS

You've probably heard that first impressions are the most important. That is particularly true when you are running a business. Much of your success will be built entirely on your reputation and image, so it pays to make this a focus.

How to Dress to Impress

Would you want a doctor to operate on you if they were dressed in jeans and a tank top? Or if they had blood on their clothes? Probably not! How you dress does matter, and it affects what your clients think of you.

For microblading, you want to look professional and clean. It is a mildly invasive procedure, which means people will expect more sterile clothing than a regular t-shirt and jeans. Most salons have a dress code or uniform, and you'll want to follow this tradition.

Your uniform should consist of:

Tunic: This can be any solid color, but a white tunic really gives the impression of a sterile, clean environment. It can be difficult to keep a white tunic clean, but it's an essential part of your job.

Pants: Slacks or dress pants can be worn, or you can use pressed scrub pants. They may be the same color as the tunic, or you may opt for a neutral color: for example, a white tunic with black pants. They should be easy to clean.

Shoes: Your shoes should be only for the salon and will ideally be white or black to match your uniform. They should be comfortable for you to spend hours wearing, but you'll also need to keep them spotless for hygiene reasons. Clients tend to feel more at ease when everything, right down to your shoes, is pristine.

Hair: Keep your hair out of the way while working to present a clean and professional image. You can use a cap to hold your hair back or invest in some hair nets.

Face Mask: Put a face mask on while working on clients, as you do not want to breathe on the open wounds. It's also a good idea to prevent any blood from getting on your face.

Salon Coat or Apron: You can put on a salon coat or apron to present the image of being clean in a salon environment. A simple solid color is best and will help you look qualified.

Your uniform says a lot about how you run your salon, so be sure that you choose something timeless and professional looking.

How to Build a Name and Reputation

You can invest in all the marketing you like, but if people aren't happy with your service, you won't get too far. In a service based industry like this, you need word of mouth. That's why it is so important to make a good first impression.

Aside from impressing people right off the bat, it's a good idea to nurture your clients. Ask them to review your business if you see they're pleased with the work. They can review on FB, Yelp, or another site where you are listed. In today's social savvy world, social media is a big part of finding salons. If people are leaving reviews and mentioning you on social media, your business can take off.

You can also encourage referrals. When a customer is happy with your work, let them know that you honor referrals. Just have the customer tell you who referred them and then offer something small, but valuable, like a discount on future work to the referrer. Send gift cards such as Starbucks gift cards to your customers who refer their friends and family to you. This will get people talking about you around town. Word of mouth is extremely effective. People trust what their friends tell them about experiences with businesses. Best of all, it's very affordable to offer incentives.

Ensure that your customers are happy by quickly fixing any potential issues. If they have a complaint, address it in a professional manner and try to make it up to them. People are often willing to talk you up if you've taken the time to listen to them and try to fix the situation.

11

How to Make the Best First Impression

That first impression, when your client steps through the door, is the most important one. What your salon looks like can make or break your reputation. However, the most important thing is cleanliness.

No one wants to stay long in a place that is perceived as dirty, so you'll need to ensure your treatment space not only looks spotless, but feels that way, too. Here are a few tips on how to make a great first impression:

Keep Colors Simple

A basic white for the room will help it feel cleaner, right from the start. If you do opt for other colors, select something that is basic and offers and sterile feel to it, like mint green or baby blue. You can add accents to make the space pop, like wall art and plants, but the underlying theme should give you an overall sense of cleanliness.

Empty the Garbage

While trash cans are useful for tossing garbage in, you should empty the can between each client. Seeing someone else's blood on a tissue is not very reassuring to the client. Trash bags are a nice and easy way to eliminate the garbage quickly. Speed the process up by leaving a bunch of extra trash bags at the bottom so you can just pull another one up and fit it immediately.

Sweep and Mop

When you sweep and mop between each client, you'll have a nice, freshly cleaned space for every person who comes in. Make sure you get the corners since small bits and debris can collect there and even a few pieces of lint in the corner of a room can make it look dirty.

Use a great smelling disinfectant on your mop to help give the space a fresh scent, too.

Wipe Everything Down

Between each client, you should also disinfect the chair you use and wipe down all surfaces. There are a number of easy to use disinfectant wipes that will help you do this quickly and easily. When a client comes in and sees that everything is glistening because it has just been wiped, they will feel comfortable letting you do their brows.

Tidy Up

It's easy to let your work table or counter get cluttered, but that looks messy and can make the client think you're unorganized. Just take a few seconds before you bring the client in and tidy your workspace. You can put instruments or tools away, restock anything that is running low and clean the mirror.

Make Your Space Smell Clean

Certain smells tend to make us think things are clean. While your salon space should smell attractive, using a lemon scent will make it smell "cleaner" to your clients. It will also help mask the scent of antiseptics that you use, which can be unpleasant.

Other scents that work well to make a good first impression include sandalwood, bergamot, lavender, and grapefruit. You can use an essential oil diffuser if you like, to keep the smells fresh. Just be careful not to mix something like pine with grapefruit or the whole space will smell horrible.

Add a Personal Touch

While sterile is good, you don't want to go too far with the clinical look. After all, you are in a salon, so up the luxury factor with some personal touches. Wall art and lighting, for example, should be on point to give a great impression.

Deal with Pests

Even the cleanest spaces can end up with ants or a mouse. If you notice anything like this, be sure to deal with it immediately. Bugs and rodents are unsanitary and can ruin your profits, as well as give a poor impression. Call an exterminator if you need to, but get rid of the problem as soon as you become aware of it.

Pay Attention to Your Look

Looking after your own personal appearance is just as important as the space. Make sure you wear your hair neatly back and have your nails done nicely, as well as your makeup if wearing any. You should also have good brows since that's what the client is there for. If your own eyebrows are a mess, they won't trust you to handle theirs. You should also use a good deodorant and keep breath mints on hand since you'll be working up close and personal with people.

Always Pay Attention to Your Surroundings

Look around your space and ask yourself if you would let someone tattoo you there. Look for anything that might give an off impression and fix it immediately.

CHAPTER 4

HOW TO PRICE YOUR SERVICES

How much money can you actually make with microblading? That depends on your clientele and who trained you. The price also depends on the skills you have, the products you use, and the value you provide to your clients.

Branding

You can double your price when you choose to brand your microblading service. If you trained with Phibrows and you have Phibrows Professional Artist Certification, your service will be more highly valued and appreciated since Phibrows is a famous brand worldwide. More and more people are starting to notice the Phibrows brand, and you can never go wrong with a strong and famous brand behind you.

How Much to Charge

Right now, microbladers are charging between $350-$800 for brows. The average is $450 and may or may not include touchups after 4-8 weeks.

While these are average prices, you should look into the salons that offer microblading in your area. They may have a different pricing system. It is possible to set the standard by creating a name for yourself, but keep in mind that it is likely to be difficult in the beginning. If you are setting up a business from scratch, you'll need to work within the confines of the competition.

Factors to Consider

Location is important since you will need to look at what others are charging around you, as well as their skill levels. In an area where you have to pay higher rent, you'll need more clients or higher prices.

Time is another factor to look at. How long does it take you to do brows? In the beginning, it will use up a lot of time. As you get more used to the process, you'll be able to finish in less time, which increases your hourly wage.

As mentioned at the beginning of this chapter, your training will determine how much you can reasonably, charge, too. But, even more importantly, experience matters. How long have you been doing this? You can charge far more over a couple months of practicing or if you have a couple years of experience.

Take a look at your costs. If you charge $350 for your services, how many clients do you need in order to pay your bills each month?

You'll have to factor in the cost of pigment, equipment payments or value, electricity, materials, rent, and your time, as well as any other overhead costs. It may end up that you don't make much money when you charge the lowest rates. If that's the case, you'll want to up your prices.

Finally, what services you offer will affect your pricing. Regular microblading is lower priced than microblading adding shading, or more complicated designs. However, if you practice and work on building those skills, you can easily charge more. You'll also increase your clientele, since more people are seeking specialty skills and are willing to pay for them.

As you build a reputation and a name for yourself, you'll eventually be able to increase your prices. Being the best microblader in town allows you to set your own prices according to demand, not competition. However, it takes time to get to that point, which is what this book can help you with.

A word of advice: In the beginning, when your skills are not advanced or perfected yet, you can charge a lesser amount to build experience. When you have built up your microblading skills and experience, you should charge a higher price since the price reflects how experienced you are.

Think about adding values to your services such as offering guarantees, providing exceptional customer service, or adding more services such as shading or powder brows to keep your price at the higher end in town. Your price in the future will determine what type of customers you have.

You are doing eyebrows, which is a really important beauty feature on the face. Customers who care about their look will research and go to the best place for their brows and will not go to the cheapest place. Charge what your work is worth, and you'll see plenty of clients.

CHAPTER 5

---✵---

HOW TO DO A MICROBLADING CONSULTATION

A microblading consultation may occur before the procedure is booked, or on the day of the procedure. It's usually best to plan ahead and have the client come in a few days before he/she gets their microblading done.

The purpose of the consultation is to find out what the client expects from the procedure and to work out which pigments you'll need, as well as selecting the correct brow shape. It's an informative session, as well. You'll let your client know exactly what to expect and explain the materials used.

Ideally, by the end of the consultation, you'll both be comfortable with moving forward.

What You Need for a Consultation

During your consultation with a client, you'll be using a few different items. Not everyone uses all of these materials, but you should be aware of them.

Know Your Craft

Be ready to explain what is a microblading process and how it is done in step by step to clients. Explain how long it will last, how the color will heal, when to expect the final result, how clients will experience during the aftercare procedure.

Have examples ready and arrange all examples in a booklet to look professional. You can get booklets printed very easily at your local print shop, and it's worth having several around so you can show ideas to one client while another browses your paste work.

Showcase Your Value

Show your clients why they should make an appointment with you instead of other salons in town. You should do competitive research of other salons around you and figure out your best assets. Write these assets down, put them in the booklet and also provide evidence or pictures as proof. Refer to chapter 10 for more information on this.

Client's Preferences

Before you even start mixing pigments or sketching you'll need to find out what the client wants from the procedure. They may have some examples of brows they love already, or you might need to guide them. Find out if they want light or dark, thin or thick, and give them some examples of what you're talking about. It's helpful to have a sample brow sheet to give them a better idea of what you can do.

Color Test

You want to make sure you have the right colors for the client's brows. You'll mix up samples of pigments and spread them on the client's forehead to get a better idea of which colors work best with their skin and hair color. You'll need a mixing palette or microblading ring for this, as well as pigments and something to pick up the pigment with. You can do the swatches with a finger.

Have Testimonials Ready

If you have testimonials or reviews, print them out in a booklet to ready to show and build trust. These may go in your portfolio or in a separate booklet. You may even want to print and frame some of the most flattering comments you've received.

Before/After Pictures

Have samples of before and after pictures to ready to show to your potential customers. You can arrange them in a booklet to look professional.

Videos

Before/after videos of previous clients are even better than photos and have a bigger impact. Have videos and pictures ready in a file in your phone or in a memory drive that is connected to a TV to showcase your work. In order to make these videos, you'll need a camera mount for your phone or someone else to record while you work.

You can also do a simple video of before and after where you have the client turn their head to provide a look at all angles.

Go Over Consent Form

After client is comfortable with moving forward, you can go over the consent form with her. You will explain what the client should expect during the procedure and after the procedure.

You will also go over the client's medical history to find out if any medical complications require consent from the client's doctor. Be thorough and professional. If there are any medical complications, ask your client to ask her/his doctor's consent before the appointment.

Be Patient

This is the time that you listen to your clients to know their needs. What they tell you will determine how happy they are with the final results. You'll need to pay close attention to what the client actually wants and direct her if you feel they would look better with something a bit different.

Ask questions such as: "What is your goal with your eyebrows?" "What shape appeals to you most?" and "Do you have examples of what you want?"

The reason is that some clients already have a lot of eyebrow hair already, but they still want a fuller look. For these clients, you don't have to do too many strokes. Instead, you make fewer strokes in areas that do not need too much and more strokes on areas where she needs more.

For clients with no eyebrows or clients with not much eyebrow hair, microblading is a way to provide the most natural eyebrows they can have. You need to be very careful when drawing the shape. You can make denser strokes for these clients.

Ask your client if she wears makeup every day and asks her for an everyday look picture. If she wears makeup a lot, then she will probably want darker, thicker, bolder eyebrows. This will give you a good idea of how to start shaping and what color pigments to use.

For clients who do not wear makeup, you want to make the eyebrows look as close to their natural eyebrows as much as possible (what we mean by this is do not draw a shape that goes outside of her natural eyebrows too much and choose a color that best matches her natural eyebrow color).

How to Make Your Consultation Materials

Most of the materials you use in your consultation can be made by you.

Keep records of all before/after pictures from past customers to build up your portfolio. As you have more customers, you can pick and choose the best works to showcase; however, in the beginning, the more pictures you have, the better you look under the customers' eyes.

Arrange your pictures in an album or booklet. You can do this by hand, printing off images and putting them in a photo album, or you can print out a customized sheet or booklet of all the eyebrow shapes and styles as a reference for customers to choose.

Make a sheet of all the colors available and ready to explain which color goes with which hair color. If the client is undecided, this is a good time to do swatches and show them what the different colors will look like with their skin tone.

The consultation is one of the most important parts of the process. Without it, you'll be flying blind. In order to get the best results and avoid mistakes, do the consult, even if it means taking 10 minutes before you start microblading.

CHAPTER 6

HOW TO PREPARE YOUR WORK AREA

Your microblading space will need to conform to the guidelines laid out by the local health department, but there are a few general things to pay attention to.

How to Set Up Your Tools

A simple table or rolling instrument tray is ideal for keeping your tools close while you work on the client. Cover the table or tray with a dental bib to keep things neat and clean. Then you can lay out all the instruments and items you'll need on the table. After every client, replace the dental bib to make the work area clean.

As you take out each of your tools, they should be sprayed or wiped with sani cloth and kept wet for at least two minutes. Everything from the brow ruler to your tweezers needs to be disinfected.

Set everything out so you can easily reach it at any point during the procedure. Usually, this means the larger or less used items will be near the back of the tray, with the smaller or more useful items at the front. Be sure to have enough cotton wipes since it can be a pain to scramble for these once you've started.

Items You'll Need During the Microblading Procedure:

- Trash container
- Alcohol wipes to clean and disinfect client's brows before procedure
- Sharps container
- Camera to take pictures
- Hair net for client and artist
- Mask
- Disposable gloves
- Ring light
- Brows pencil
- Eyebrows ruler
- Tweezers
- Eyebrows scissors
- Pigment
- Anesthetics
- Wet cotton wipes
- Dry cotton wipes
- Disposable blade

How to Maintain Sanitation During the Microblading Process

While microblading doesn't require absolute sterility, sanitation is essential to avoid infection. Scrub your hands with soap and water before you begin the procedure and don gloves. You should also wear a face mask to prevent breathing into the fresh cuts.

As you work, be careful not to contaminate anything. For example, your pigments should be mixed ahead of time and the pigment containers stored.

Sanitizing the Client

Use alcohol antiseptic to disinfect the client's hands. While they shouldn't be touching their face, it sometimes happens, and if it does, you want to be sure they have clean hands.

Before beginning work, of course, you'll be cleaning the client's skin with alcohol antiseptic. Be very thorough about this to prevent any extra bacteria from getting into the cuts. It's good practice to clean all around the client's forehead and brow, even areas you won't be microblading, since your gloved hands will be touching these areas. Avoid transferring bacteria from other areas.

A hair net will prevent the client's hair from getting tangled in your hands or touching the brows while you are working on them.

Re-Gloving

If you need to stop and remix pigments or interrupt your microblading session for any reason, peel your gloves off from the wrist, discard, and wash your hands. Once you've finished with your task, you should wash your hands again and don fresh gloves.

Disposal Practices

As you use instruments, drop them into a kidney bowl if they are to be reused, like the brow ruler. These will need to be properly sanitized later. Drop any garbage into a bin as soon as you finish with it, such as wipes, cotton wipes, etc. Anything sharp needs to be discarded in the actual sharps container.

Other Tips

Set out everything you need ahead of time, so you don't have to interrupt your session too often. Its fine to take a break, but rummaging around in the cupboard for instruments or supplies you should have had out will make things more difficult and less sanitary.

You should have sanitary procedures from when you were training, but it never hurts to improve on them. Keep everything clean and make sure you wipe down all surfaces between clients and sweep and empty the garbage. This will not only keep things clean, but it will also give your clients a better impression.

CHAPTER 7

HOW TO MAKE YOUR PORTFOLIO

A portfolio is the best way to show potential clients what your work looks like. You should take before and after photos of every client who agrees to it. However, there's a lot more to creating a great portfolio than snapping a quick photo before you start. You want professional images to showcase your professional work.

How to Grow Your Portfolio

How do you get clients to let you take images in the first place? You can start during the training period. You'll have people who are willing to let you try your techniques on them under the watchful eye of your instructor, so it's the perfect time to start collecting photos. If you mess up at all, you don't need to use those images.

Once your training is done, you can build your portfolio by offering discounts to new clients, or coupons and free services in exchange for referrals. This will help bring more people in to get their brows done. The more clients you have, the faster your portfolio will grow.

How to Take Before/After Pictures

The before and after photos are necessary to show potential clients exactly your talents. You can show people the after shots, but it really helps to see what the difference is between the before and after. That's where the real test is . . . how much you've improved clients' eyebrows.

What Equipment You Need For Pictures

High-quality images are easy enough to get, but you'll need some specific equipment. It's best to invest in this early on because it will help you get more clients in the long run.

Camera: You don't need an actual camera, but you do need a very good phone camera. One of the later iPhones or a high-quality Android can work well.

Ring Light: A ring light is easy to pick up, and it will make all the difference in your photos. The ring light provides good, even lighting that will showcase the brows you work on.

Backdrop: This can be a wall or a sheet that you hang up to take the picture against. You want to have consistent backgrounds in order to show the results unaltered. Ideally, your backdrop will be solid in color. White is the best option.

If you can't get a proper light, natural light from the window can work, if you have a reflector on the opposite side. A reflector can be as simple as a white wall or a large piece of white poster board.

Choosing the Best Angle

It might seem obvious to take a straight-on a photograph of the client's brows. Facing the camera directly makes it easy to see the arch of the brow. The eyes should be at camera level when you take the photo.

Once you have the brows finished, you can redo the front view photo, but it's also a good idea to snap a ¾ angle view of the brows. This will give people a better idea of how the brows look from the side, while still providing a good view.

Having your clients lay down when taking the pictures will produce better photos. Arrange the camera in a way to have clients look directly into the camera.

Always check in your phone for the best angle that will produce the best shape because you will notice that the eyebrows will look different from different angles.

Advice When Taking Before/after Pictures:

Always take a lot of pictures. Sometimes, we take 20 pictures before we pick out the best one. You only showcase the best picture, don't show everything.

Apps You Need

A couple of apps will help you get the results you want for your portfolio.

PhiApp: Developed to help you create perfect brows, this app is a good way to ensure brows are symmetrical at the drawing stage.

Picsart: Use this app to edit your photos for clarity and to create simple photo collages to make your before and after images shine. When you have Phibrows logo, you can use this app to add logo into your photo. Use add photo option, then pick blend, then pick multiply will produce a nice logo into the photo without the white background.

Canva: This online image compiler allows you to design your brochures, as well as create photo collages to showcase yours before and after images. We recommend using this tool when you have some basics computer skills or some graphic design knowledge already.

How to Watermark Your Work

Both the Picsart Photo Editor and Canva will let you add a watermark to your photos. This could be as simple as your company name, or you might want to add a logo, as well. Make it mostly transparent so it won't be obtrusive. This will help protect you from others stealing your photos and using them as their own.

To add the PhiBrows logo to your work, use the add photo option, then pick blend, then pick multiply will produce a nice logo into the photo without the white background.

With a handful of before and after photos, you can easily create your portfolio, but the more options you have, the better. Not only can you add these to your social media, but you can use them in your brochures and other advertising materials.

Your portfolio may be in paper form, as well as on your website. Ideally, you'll have a wide variety of brow shapes and colors to show people. The more experience you have, the bigger and better your portfolio will be.

If you don't have a Phibrows logo, you can also watermark your works with your salon's contact info.

CHAPTER 8

HOW TO DEAL WITH UNHAPPY CLIENTS

In every business, you're bound to get an unhappy client once in a while. Unfortunately, that may be even more common with service industries and particularly one like microblading, where it has to do with the client's appearance. An unhappy client can destroy your reputation, so it's important to have a plan for when this happens.

No one wants an unhappy client, but sometimes, your customer may just be the complaining type, always finding something wrong with any service they receive. If this is the case, you'll end up with complaints even if the job goes perfectly.

When this happens, your best bet is to make the client happy by reducing your price or offering something small for free and then refusing to work with them if they call again. You can also talk to other services in the area to learn who to avoid.

How to Avoid Messing Up Clients' Eyebrows

First, you need to be sure you have enough training that you'll be comfortable working on people's brows and tougher cases. The more practice you get, the better you'll be and the more likely you'll be able to handle.

Always have clients sign a consent form to educate your clients what to expect from a microblading procedure.

Communication is key. This is why you need to have consultations before you actually start working on the client's face. What you might think is ideal may not be exactly what your client wants. It's up to you to verify their needs and be sure to understand what they have in mind.

Do a Patch Test

Ask about any allergies or health issues before starting. You should also do a small test to make sure the client won't have any adverse reaction. Many horror stories come about because the person is allergic to something in the pigment. Patch test will let you know if this is an issue before you have to deal with a full-blown allergy. You should also know exactly what is in your pigments so you can decide if they are safe to use for someone with specific allergies.

However, you'll also need to do a patch test, to ensure the patient isn't allergic once you start using the blades.

What do you test in a Patch Test?

You should test:

Pigment: some customers might be allergic to ingredients in the pigments used

Blade: some customers might be allergic to materials in the blade you use

Anesthetics: some customers might be allergic to anesthetics

How to Do a Patch Test:

At least 48 hours before the procedure, have client come in for a patch test. Make 1 tiny stroke with blade with pigment on the right ear and 1 tiny stroke with anesthetics on the left ear. If you notice the cut is really red or swollen or has pus coming from the stroke within 24-48 hours, you should avoid doing the microblading procedure for the client. You should also ask if they have an itchy, burning pain sensation, which also indicates a bad reaction. Again, don't perform microblading if the client is experiencing any of these feelings in the areas that were tested.

What to Do When Things Go Wrong

You should know how to correct the most common problems that occur with microblading.

The most common problems with microblading include clients not liking shape, color, or strokes. Your training provider should train you how to fix these mistakes already.

If you can't do much more to fix the brow and make it the way your client wants, there are other options:

Put yourself in the client's shoes and figure out a way to make them feel better.

Offer a free follow up session to adjust the brows in 4 weeks. You can also give a discount on the service you provided, or even refuse payment if the problem is very bad.

If the client is merely annoyed with the fact that the brows look different than they had anticipated, but you didn't actually do anything wrong, it's still a good idea to make them feel better by offering a gift certificate for secondary service (hair, lashes, or whatever else you offer at your salon), or a discount on the next time they do their brows with you.

Unhappy customers may or may not be legit, but either way, they can leave a bad review and cause issues for your business. This is particularly damaging in the beginning when you are trying to get started, so try to avoid making anyone unhappy.

Handling Bad Reviews

What should you do if you do get a bad review? Online reputation management is something every business owner has to deal with at some point. You can either handle it yourself, or you can pay someone to do it for you.

Online reputation management is basically ensuring that the good reviews get to the top of the search results. This requires staying on top of what people are saying about you. Set up a Google Alert for your business name and you'll get notified every time something pops up about you, good or bad.

If some of the bad reviews do show up, you want to have people discount them as much as possible. This is best done by getting the good reviews to rate higher. So, when you get a good review, share it on all social media accounts.

The simplest method of refuting a bad review is to offer a fix. If someone seemed fine when they left your salon, but complained about your service on a forum or social media, you could respond publicly.

Apologize for the issue and offer a way to fix it, even if it's just coming back for a touchup free of cost. Be polite and never get into an argument online. Anyone coming across the bad review will immediately see that you are reacting in a positive manner and that counts in your favor.

Whatever you do, don't engage in angry insults and emails or messages. These can and will be used against you and your business, so you want to remain professional at all times.

CHAPTER 9

HOW TO GET TESTIMONIALS

Your portfolio is important, but testimonials are social proof that you do great work. The simplest way to get these is to just ask. If your client is happy, ask them if they'd be willing to write a quick endorsement. You can even make it easy for them by providing a list of brief questions.

Asking isn't the only way, though! Try checking on social media to see if anyone has mentioned your business in a favorable light. You can share tweets on your website, or you can take a screenshot of the comment and post it.

You can send out an email, as well, to all your previous clients and ask them to take a short survey. Ask a few questions and have the last one be a request for a testimonial, or ask permission to use their responses. For example, you might ask "what was the best part of using our service?" The client's response could easily become a great testimonial.

Other places to collect testimonials include:

- Blog comments
- Emails

- Satisfaction cards
- Verbal responses (request they write it down)
- Via a testimonial app on your site

Remember, it's always best to get permission to use the testimonial. This will eliminate any potential issues in the future.

What Makes a Great Testimonial

Someone saying they like your service is nice, but it's not the kind of testimonial you want. A great testimonial will be honest, but also give specifics. For example, the client might elaborate on how they appreciated your attention to details, how clean the room was, or how you turned non-existent brows into something incredible. Details matter.

Not only are details important, but the testimonial will look better if you can use a photo and/or name with it. You should also have permission to use the testimonial.

How to Present Testimonials

Testimonials can be in written form or in video format. You'll want to put them on your website, of course, but there are other places to use great testimonials.

Website: On your site, scatter the testimonials throughout your copy, particularly anywhere people might find it difficult to justify using your services. As an example, if you show prices, add a testimonial that talks about how affordable or how worth it your service is.

Social media: Share tidbits from your testimonials on social media. These can be designed for the specific platform they'll be on. Instagram does really well with short quotes over an image, while Facebook is a great place to share video reviews.

Email: When you send out an email about a new service, price change, etc. why not include a couple testimonials from happy clients? This helps reinforce the fact that you are a professional who can do a great job on their brows.

Printed Materials: Your marketing materials can benefit from a well-placed testimonial or two. These are a great way to boost credibility, particularly in brochures. Don't overwhelm potential clients with them, but a couple of quotes can be useful. Some salons create a booklet that is only based on testimonials.

Guest Book: Set up a guest book for your clients to sign after they've had their procedure. You can then pull the best testimonials from what they write down in the book. This also lets other clients look at what people have written.

Testimonials are the best way to let potential clients know that you are good at what you do. People trust other people who have had good experiences with a salon, so this is a great way to increase trust.

CHAPTER 10

HOW TO MAKE YOUR MICROBLADING SERVICE UNIQUE

Don't just wait for clients to show up to your door. It is your responsibility to work it, to bring in clients, and to encourage clients to spread the word. This will decide if you will be successful or not. People who are successful work harder. They don't just get lucky, and all their clients don't just magically come into their salons.

You aren't the only microblading service available, so you'll need to stand out a bit in order to get clients. How do you make your service unique enough that people will want to come to you?

Check out your competition and notice what they do well and what they mess up. You can read reviews on their services and learn from them. Then make sure your service is better.

For example, if customers complain about how surly the staff is, make sure you are friendlier. If they say something about how the salon doesn't offer shading, make sure you do. You can learn a lot from your competition and offer better services to your clients. This is the best way to ensure people start coming to your salon instead of visiting others.

Adding Value to Your Microblading Service

After you have researched your competitors' services and offers, write down a list. Find out what areas are your stronger areas and write them down. The areas might include:

Which Products You Use

What brand of pigments you use (using correct pigment is the most important feature in deciding the healed result. If you use Phibrows pigments, your work will not heal into red, purple, or blue gray (as long as you have correct stroke depth).

If you use Phibrows Measuring Divider and PhiApp, you will have a clear mapping of the eyebrows with measuring lines to show to your clients that their eyebrows are perfectly even before doing the procedure. This will give you a significant advantage over your competitors, and you make sure you show this during the consultation to increase the chance of clients booking with you.

Offer guarantees such as customers' eyebrows will not heal red or purple (give examples of red eyebrows and purple eyebrows). You should have a sheet that shows how the eyebrows can be ruined if someone isn't good at what they do.

If you are confident and always have good healed result, you should point this out to your clients with your healing pictures. Get these photos by asking clients to come in for a checkup. You can offer them a little extra something like a gift card with an expiration date

If you can fix bad eyebrows that turned red or blue, or purple, mention this as an added value, you will provide to your client. In fact, any kind of repair you can do will bring you more clients.

Focus on these values when you do advertisements.

Areas that need to be addressed in order to make your service amazing:

Pricing: Some people opt for the cheapest option, but that doesn't mean you need to offer the lowest prices. Once you have a reputation, you should be able to raise your rates. However, you should always make sure that your work is well worth the price you charge.

Space: Where you do the microblading will also have an impact on what people think of your company. If someone walks in and there are bloody tissues in the wastebasket and dirt on the floor or gloves lying around, they won't feel safe. We covered this under making a good first impression, but it bears repeating.

Some microblading salons function out of a house. That's fine, as long as the room you use is neat and tidy and follows the sanitation guidelines laid out by the local health center as well as the place is permitted by the health department. Make a good impression, and you'll be recommended to others.

Results: While all other factors help the client decide whether or not they like you and your space, the final result is what will make or break the whole thing. Mess up someone's brows, and they'll be upset, or even angry. However, if you do an excellent job, you'll find yourself inundated with clients, often just from word of mouth.

Customer Service: How you treat people will have a massive bearing on whether or not they give a good review or recommend your services to others. Even if you are the best microblader in town, no one will visit you if you're difficult to work with or snap at people and treat them poorly.

You can increase your customer service rating by greeting customers with a smile and chatting with them as you get ready for the procedure. Keep a warm look on your face.

As you work with new clients, you'll find that they have good suggestions for improving your service to them, so pay attention. Some of this information may come from reviews, while you can also ask your clients what you can do to better serve them.

Going Over and Above

To really impress your clients, you can take things up a notch. Offer a cold drink before you begin, or use aromatherapy in your salon. Simple things like this can help people select your salon over someone else's.

Get back to your customers quickly, too. If they call and leave a message, try to return the call within half an hour. This increases the chances of landing the appointment. People love prompt responses.

If you don't currently have a website, you definitely need to set one up. This is an essential part of being found online and can make all the difference.

After all, if someone checks Google Maps for a microblading salon and finds five, but yours is the only one with a website, they will choose you. They can jump onto your site and find out exactly what you offer and how you will provide the services.

Something else you should keep in mind is who your ideal client is. Are you looking to reach young women who want to be as stylish as possible? Or are you focusing on older women with thinning hair and possible health issues? Knowing who your ideal customer is will help you cater directly to them. You're also more likely to make your clients happy when you know exactly what they need and provide it.

Ideally, you will provide better service and a better microblading experience than anyone else in your area. It's a matter of paying attention to what your clients want and what your competitors offer. If you are providing what people need and your competition isn't, then you'll always be a standout in your field.

There are so many ways to make your business unique, so embrace the difference and focus on the client.

CHAPTER 11

IMPORTANT BASIC MARKETING PRINCIPLES EVERY MICROBLADING ARTIST MUST FOLLOW FOR SUCCESS

Now that you know how much to charge and how to handle a microblading consultation, how do you promote your business?

The first thing you need to do is look into marketing materials. Many of these can be created at home, but if you have the budget, hire a graphic artist. A professional can turn out amazing products in a very short time and will give you exactly what you need.

Logo

Before you start with any major promo, you should have a logo and business colors. There's no right way to do this, but your logo should represent your values and standards. It's usually worth investing some cash in this. After all, the logo will represent your company for the next several years, if not longer.

Colors are also important. What colors best represent your business? Stay away from boring hues, like brown or olive. Aim for colors that make you feel fresh and beautiful since that's how you want your customers to feel. You'll want two colors, possibly with an accent color. Avoid mixing too many, as that can get confusing.

If you have an existing salon, you'll probably already have both colors and a logo to work with.

What Marketing Materials Do You Need?

Having marketing materials to hand out will make it that much simpler for people to understand the value of your service and to make it easy for people to get in touch with you. They'll see exactly what you offer, which is an important part of advertising.

Brochures

A brochure is usually a trifold paper, but it can also be a small booklet that you can offer potential clients. This should outline what services you offer, usually with prices, and give people an idea of what to expect.

For example, you might include a few before and after photos to let people know what microblading looks like, a price list for your services, and a basic description of how microblading works.

Even if you offer other services, you may want a brochure just on the microblading side of things.

Business Cards

Business cards are really a must-have. Even if you choose to do nothing else, you'll want to have business cards made up. It's possible to make your own and print them off on your home printer, but that's not recommended. Your business card represents your entire business and should be just as sleek and professional as you are. Home printed cards tend to be a little uneven once cut, and they can be lower quality, as well. To give the best impression, you should have a printer do them up.

Cards need to include your logo, contact info, name, and should also include what you offer, just as a reminder. You can include further information, but the basics will suffice and keep the card uncluttered.

Gift Certificates

If you want to boost your business, offer gift certificates. These don't have to be fancy, but they should include your logo in the upper left corner, as well as contact information. Remember that the person receiving the gift certificate may not know where you are located.

You can either create gift certificates that have a pre-determined purchase amount on them, such as $25, $50, or $100, or you can just include a space to write the amount. The blank options are more easily adjusted to the client's needs.

Give $20, $25, $30, or even $50 gift certificates to customers who love the eyebrows you just created. Give these gift certificates an expiration date so that the clients have to book within 1 month or 3 months. They will surely give these gift certificates to their friends and family. This is a good way for them to refer clients to you and will encourage new clients to try out your service. No one wants to turn down a special deal like this.

Loyalty Cards

Reward your clients for being loyal to you. If they come to you for all their microblading and/or salon needs, they should be rewarded. Loyalty cards are a good way to do that.

With a loyalty card, the client gets one visit stamped or punched each time they come, and when they've reached a certain amount, they get a discount or a free service. You can choose what you want to provide, but it can be something relatively small, but with good solid value for the client.

You can stamp the cards with each visitor per dollar amount spent.

Referral Cards

These cards make it easy and motivating for your existing clients to invite more people to your salon. They are essentially business cards that have a space in the card to write name and contact info of the person that you hand the referral cards too.

When your client hands out these referral cards to their reach of people and customers come into your salon with the cards, make a note of who sent them. You then notify the client how many customers they have referred to you and send her/him a Starbucks gift card or a check.

Earning something in return for referring people will really encourage your existing clients to get those referral cards out there. Make sure you give several to every client you have that is happy with their brows.

Booking Cards

We highly recommend to always book your client for a following service (a touchup in 4 weeks or a touchup in a year) before they walk out the door. Pre-booking clients ensure your schedule is organized and your appointment book is filled up. Having a booking card to hand out is a professional way to remind clients of their appointment.

In addition to the booking card, you may want to follow up with an email or phone call a few days before their appointment. People can and do lose booking cards, so it's helpful to have another way to contact them. This also ensures they show up for their appointment and you don't lose scheduling time.

How to Make Your Marketing Materials

If you want to do your own marketing materials, you'll need to have some basic graphic art skills. If you don't, consider hiring a professional. That being said, many people manage very well with the apps mentioned below.

Adobe Photoshop and Illustrator are what most pros use, but you don't need to get that fancy. A good option that you can use for free online is **Canva**. It lets you design whatever you want, selecting the size and you can upload images.

PicMonkey is a good option for editing images if you need more capabilities than **Canva** offers. Together, these two sites can give you nice, professional results.

You will also need good quality images. For print, you have to have 300 dpi, which means low-resolution images will not work well. They'll look blurred, pixelated, or worse.

Images can be chosen from your own portfolio, or you can use stock photos from royalty-free sites. Be sure they can be used for commercial use before adding them to your brochures. Never, ever copy images from the internet without knowing you have permission to use them for commercial use. The photographer can come after you and sue you for using unauthorized images. It's best to build up your own portfolio as quickly as possible.

Gift cards and loyalty cards are relatively easy to make up, and you can just look at sample designs online to find a good example. From there, you'll be able to create your own personalized version to use.

It does take some work to create truly professional materials to use for marketing, but it's important to get it right. You want to give a professional impression, and that starts with your printed marketing materials.

CHAPTER 12

HOW TO MAKE YOUR BUSINESS KNOWN

It doesn't matter how good you are at microblading if no one knows you exist. Getting your business out there is a big part of establishing a salon. It's not enough to let friends and family know that you are offering your services; you need to go bigger. Fortunately, today's technology makes that remarkably easy.

Online Techniques

Build a Website

You can either create a website on your own or have someone else do it for you, but it's almost a requirement in the industry to have your own website. You don't need anything too fancy, but you should have a page set up to give people basic information about your services.

Your site should use local keywords, such as "your town microblading" or "your town tattoo makeup" and others. This will help Google show your pages when people search for those terms. It's also important to include contact information.

Ideally, your website will have the following pages:

Home: Give some information about the business and what you do. It should be a general introduction, though you can go into what services you offer if you like.

About/Contact: This page will give more information about you. It should include where you studied, any extra certifications you hold, and how many years of experience you have. This page should also have your contact information (although your phone number should be at the bottom of the site anyway, no matter which pages the person is on). You may include a map or contact form here, as well, or you might want to separate the two sections and have another page just for contact.

Reviews/Testimonial: This is the page that you put all of your reviews and testimonials. You can showcase testimonials by videos or quotes from your customers. Be sure to include customers' name and pictures.

Gallery/Portfolio: This is where you will feature your portfolio of before and after photos. People will check this page to see what you've done previously. It can help them make a decision as to whether or not they want to hire you.

Services: What services do you offer? This page is where you will list the various options and possibly your pricing model.

Blog: This is the section where you'll provide clients with updates on the business, information on your services and share about microblading in general. Blog posts are also good for building an online presence and give you something extra to share on social media sites.

Privacy Policy: Every site needs one of these pages for legal reasons. The good news is that you can easily generate one online and add it. A privacy policy protects you from getting in trouble, and it is non-negotiable.

Email Sign Up: This doesn't need to be a full page on its own, but you definitely need a place where people can sign up for your newsletter. You can offer this service as a popup or include it in your sidebar and posts. Make sure the form is available on every single page of the website.

If you use Wordpress, you can add a plugin that will let people book online. There are a number of these available, so choose one that works well for your needs.

Use Google Maps

Often the first thing people do when looking for a specific service is search on Google. For local searches, Google Maps will usually pop up first in the results, with a list of local choices. You can make sure you're on this list by going to Google My Business and adding your salon. It's helpful to have a website so you can direct people there, but at the very least, include a phone number and address.

Encourage happy customers to rate you on Google Maps and to upload their own photos. This can help build your reputation, and more people will see your site.

Use Facebook

In order to promote your business on Facebook, you'll need to set up a business page first. You can do this from your own profile there. Make sure your logo is clearly visible on the page. Usually, it's a good idea to make your logo the profile image, so it will show up everywhere you leave a comment.

Be sure to fill in all the contact information and write a short blurb about the business. Basically, you want to give people all the information they need in order to decide to book with you. And speaking of booking, you should have the button on the upper right part of the Facebook Page set to go to your booking app or website. Make it very easy for anyone visiting the page to get a consultation.

Use Instagram

Instagram is a rapidly growing social media site that relies heavily on images. That makes it an excellent option for your salon. You can post before and after photos, special offers, and grand opening announcements there.

For Instagram, you'll need square photos, so it often works best to take two horizontal brow images and put them together with an app like PicsArt to create a square image that will fit perfectly with Instagram.

Of course, while people want to see brow photos, they aren't going to follow your account for just that, so make sure you include other fun images. Behind the scenes, shots of your space or work will also do well, and you can include customer testimonies over a simple background as an image, as well.

When writing your descriptions, be sure to use hashtags. These will help people find your pictures, and they'll start looking through them and follow you. For example, you might tag a brow image with #phibrows or #microblading. You can use up to 30 hashtags, so be sure to use all the relevant ones.

Use Pinterest

Another very hot social media site these days is Pinterest. If you want people to notice you, it's the best place to be, aside from Instagram. You can "pin" images to boards you create. It's also possible to set up a business account and even to schedule pins, so you don't need to be on there all the time.

In addition to sharing your blog posts and portfolio images, you can get new ideas for microblading from Pinterest. There are many beauty accounts there and people searching for more information. If you have it, share it.

Pinterest works best if you are posting on a daily basis. You should also pin other people's pins here and there and make a point of following other accounts. Join group boards to really maximize the effect of your pins. More people will see them when you pin to a group board. Most will have instructions on how to join in the board description.

Hire an Influencer

Influencers are people who are very active on social media, have a large fan following and are great at reviewing or recommending worthwhile products and services. They hire out their accounts to companies like yours and will recommend your salon for a fee. It's usually well worth it since you can reach a lot of interested people.

Offline Techniques

If you want to promote your business these days, you can also benefit from offline techniques also. There are plenty of offline opportunities, though and these can also be great for finding new clients. You might try one or more of the following:

Radio Ads

Does your town have a local radio station? If so, call them up and find out how much they charge for a 30 or 60-second spot. Even a simple radio ad can bring plenty of people into your salon.

Newspaper Ads

The local paper is a great place to let people know about your microblading services. Try offering them on a large ad in the middle or front of the newspaper, rather than the classifieds section. Be sure your ad is marketing to the right audience and be consistent. When people see the same ad over and over again, they begin to think they need it.

Flyers

Leaving flyers with a discount code on cars can be a fun way to reach new people. You can hire people to leave the flyers, so you aren't spending hours walking around. Alternatively, you could hand them out in a popular venue, like a fall fair.

TV Spots

Your local television channel will have ad spots available, and these can be fairly affordable, depending on where you live. Make sure you create a high-quality video ad to reach potential clients in your area.

You should always be on the lookout for ways to get your business out there. If something comes up, jump on it and make sure you take a chance. You never know when you might get a big influx of clients, thanks to your efforts.

CHAPTER 13

How to Run Online/Offline Promotions

Beyond word of mouth and social media, you will need to run promotions to help build your business.

Online Ad Campaigns

Running an ad campaign can take many different forms. Will you use online or offline services? Are you going to use an influencer or rely on a regular paid ad? Let's take a closer look at what those entail.

Social Media Ads

Social media is very hot for ads right now, but you have two choices here. You can either create an ad and pay for the platform to display it as a sponsored post, or you can pay someone with a large following to mention your business.

Influencers can be pricy, but they are also very effective. They already have a large number of people who pay close attention and repost everything they say. An ad with someone like this can end up increasing your business fairly fast. Pricing and reach will depend on who the influencer is. You will want to look for local social media celebrities since they will have quite a few followers in the area.

While ads are a little more affordable in most cases, they don't have the same impact as someone personally recommending your services. There are influencers on every social media site, you just need to ask them their rates.

If you don't know how to do it, hire a professional to do for you.

Advertise on blogs and other websites

Aside from social media, you can advertise on blogs and other websites. These could be banner or display ads that show up at the side of the blog or throughout the content, or you can have the blogger write a special post about your business. It's even possible to write the post yourself and pay the person to run it on their page.

Like influencer ads, sponsored posts tend to have better results than display ads. They show up as someone endorsing your services, which is always a bonus.

If you don't know how to do it, hire a professional to do for you.

Offline Ad Campaigns

Print Ads

You can also purchase ads in print magazines, newspapers, and other publications. As long as these are getting in front of your ideal customer, print can be a good option. Look for local publications that fit your target market if you want to reach more people. It's particularly good to create ads based around events and holidays.

New Client Promotion

Bringing in new clients is an ongoing project, but you can make it easier by offering first time customers a special deal. You might make it a discount, or you could offer another service for half price.

Alternatively, get your existing clients to bring in their friends by providing them with a discount for every referral.

Holiday Promotions

Holidays can be a wonderful way to get more clients if you plan ahead. There are two ways to do this.

First, you can promote a special offer to your clients and potential clients. For example, you might give a free lash lift to everyone who comes in for microblading. A freebie, 2 for 1 deal, or discount can bring people rushing to redeem the offer.

Second, you can promote your gift certificates. This is a great time for people to buy certificates as gifts. This type of promotion can really work well before holidays like Christmas and Valentine's Day.

Birthday Promotions

Have clients sign up for your email list in order to register their birthdays. Then give them a coupon to spend on their birthday! This kind of gift is minor for you, but it makes a big difference to your patrons, and they'll remember it. In fact, it's likely they'll share their experience.

Another option could be to offer a draw each month for anyone born in that month. In order to participate, people would need to share the information or post, resulting in better publicity for your business.

Keep an eye out for opportunities to boost visibility. Social media is a great start, but you can also use your billboards and online ads to create a bigger, better campaign for the holidays.

CHAPTER 14

---— ❧ —---

How to Use Advanced Marketing Techniques

Once you have the basics of marketing down, it's time to take things up a notch. You can go beyond the simpler methods of social media and local ads to create a bigger presence in the world, both online and off.

How to Use Press Releases to Your Advantage

As a local business, press releases can really help you get noticed. First, you'll need something announce. This could be anything from a new hire or location to a grand opening. If you participate in the community, these events can also be news worthy.

A good press release will be well written, with a quote from you included. All information people need to know about your business, and the news should also be included. Usually, the news is included in the first three paragraphs, with a final paragraph that covers your actual business.

Once you have a press release in hand, whether you wrote it yourself or hired a professional to do it, you need to distribute. There are several online options for this, which you might want to use, but it's also a good idea to send the press release with a brief cover letter to your local news outlets.

News outlets may include:

- Television
- Radio
- Newspapers
- Small magazines
- Local blogs

Anyone who might consider sharing your news should be contacted. A simple, personalized cover letter will let them know why you feel they might want to publish the information.

When a news channel picks up the information, make sure you link to it or mention on your own forums that you've been promoted on. This could be on your own social media, blog, or other outlet.

Not only does getting a shout out means you get more publicity, but it also increases your expertise level. People will often choose a salon that has been featured on multiple outlets over one that has no outside links.

How to Use Grand Openings or Grand Reopenings to Bring in Clients

Planning an opening? Make it a big one and get some serious publicity that will help boost your business. People love grand openings, and even if you have been in business for a while, you can create a grand reopening.

The idea here is to let people know that you're available and what services you offer. It's also a way to integrate your business into the local community. A grand opening can be as simple as putting up some balloons and streamers and offering cake and discounts, or it could be a huge affair with entertainment and live music, etc. The choice is yours.

Getting Publicity

If no one knows about your big event, they won't show up. That's why it's important to make a big deal of it a few weeks before you hold the opening. Send event invites to any existing clients. You should also:

Send out press releases: See above on how to do that effectively.

Create an event on FB: Make sure you submit it to any local events pages.

Promote via social media: You can even offer a contest to get people to share.

Take out an ad: A classified ad or an ad in the local newspaper announcing the event will also get more attention.

You should have a plan long before the actual day so you can promote what you're offering. Giveaways, draws, live music, food, etc. can all be ways to get people to come over. You can also offer free consultations for your microblading services.

It's also a good idea to give out business cards and, if possible, get people to sign up for your mailing list. A giveaway or coupon option can help get them to sign up. This ensures you can contact them in the future.

Planning a Reopening

A reopening is much like a grand opening, but it happens after you've been in business for a while. Usually, this will be held after you've changed locations or undergone renovations that required closing for a while.

Aside from being a second opening, this type of event should be held just like a regular grand opening.

How to Set Up a Billboard

If you really want to get noticed, a huge billboard can be a good way to go. These can be pricey, but they are also very noticeable, and many companies find that the expense is well worth it. Still, this may be something you want to do once your business is up and running well.

Most billboard companies list their numbers either on the front of an available billboard or on the back. Call this to get prices.

You'll have to plan out an image to place on the billboard. A graphic artist can help with this and will design the ad to be large enough and high enough quality that it can be printed out for that size. Keep in mind that the image has to be eye-catching, with minimal, impactful text. People will be reading it as they fly by in their cars, so you need to get the information across fast.

These advanced marketing methods are just a few of the ways you can build up your publicity. Ongoing campaigns tend to be more effective than a one-time event, though something like a grand opening can really draw a lot of people.

Author Biography

Thuong Dang and Jocelyn Tran are one of the first Phibrows Masters in the US. They have a PhiAcademy in Fresno, California training Phibrows Microblading, Phicontour Lips and Eyeliners, Powder Brows and various Phi Techniques to students all over United States. For over the years, they have been helping many students succeed and changing their lives with a career in microblading and permanent makeup.

43878179R00039

Made in the USA
Columbia, SC
23 December 2018